BEGINNING SOLO GUITAR

ARNIE BERLE & MARK GALBO

Master the "chord melody" style and play the guitar as a solo instrument!

T0080133

Amsco Publications
A Part of **The Music Sales Group**
New York/London/Paris/Sydney/Copenhagen/Berlin/Tokyo/Madrid

Cover photography by Randall Wallace
Project Editor: David Bradley
Interior design and layout by Len Vogler

CD produced by Mark Galbo

Order No. AM987382
ISBN-13: 978-0-8256-3596-0

Exclusive Distributors:
Music Sales Corporation
257 Park Avenue South, New York, NY 10010 USA

Music Sales Limited
14-15 Berners Street, London W1T 3LJ England

Music Sales Pty. Limited
20 Resolution Drive, Caringbah, NSW 2229 Australia

Printed in the United States of America by
Vicks Lithograph and Printing Corporation

I want to dedicate this book to my wife Rosalie for her patience and encouragement. Next, I want to dedicate this book to my children Norman, Nancy, Lisa, Sharon, and Barbara. I wrote all my books to feed them and keep a roof over their heads. I also want to dedicate this book to my grandchildren Zachary, Danny, David, Melissa, Jacob, and my newest grandchild Connor, to show them I can still write a book and that they can be proud of their grandfather.

Arnie Berle

Contents

Contents

6 CD Track List

1. Tuning Notes
2. C Major Scale
3. D Dorian Mode
4. G Mixolydian Mode
5. C Major Scale with I, IIm, and V7 Chords
6. F Major Scale
7. G Dorian Mode
8. C Mixolydian Mode
9. F Major Scale with I, IIm, and V7 Chords
10. G Major Scale
11. A Dorian Mode
12. D Mixolydian Mode
13. G Major Scale with I, IIm, and V7 Chords
14. Root Position Chord Scale
15. First Inversion Chord Scale
16. Second Inversion Chord Scale
17. Major Triads (1st-string melody note)
18. Minor Triads (1st-string melody note)
19. Dominant 7ths (1st-string melody note)
20. Frère Jacques (original melody)
21. Frère Jacques (melody up an octave)
22. Frère Jacques in F (chord solo)
23. Frère Jacques in F (chord solo—slow)
24. Major Triads (2nd-string melody note)
25. Minor Triads (2nd-string melody note)
26. Dominant 7ths (2nd-string melody note)
27. Frère Jacques in D (chord solo)
28. Frère Jacques in D (chord solo—slow)
29. Red River Valley (chord solo)
30. Red River Valley (chord solo—slow)
31. Cmaj7
32. Major 7th Chords (1st-string melody note)
33. Dm7
34. Minor 7th Chords (1st-string melody note)
35. Aura Lee (chord solo)
36. Earth Angel (chord solo)
37. Major 7th Chords (2nd-string melody note)
38. Minor 7th Chords (2nd-string melody note)
39. Londonderry Air (chord solo)
40. A Natural Minor Scale
41. A Harmonic Minor Scale
42. A Melodic Minor Scale
43. Greensleeves (chord solo)
44. Diminished 7th Chords
45. Everything Happens To Me (chord solo)
46. This Little Light Of Mine (melody only)
47. All Through The Night (melody only)
48. Jacob, Drink (melody only)

I first met Arnie Berle in 1988 when I went to study guitar with him at his studio in Yonkers, New York. At the time, he was still writing for *Guitar Player* magazine and I remember being quite nervous driving to my first lesson. Having read his *Guitar Player* column for years, I knew he was a famous educator and I had built up a sort of anxious anticipation over meeting him. At the first lesson, Arnie immediately put me at ease and brought a professional focus to our lesson that I knew could only have a positive effect on me.

As the first lessons passed and the weeks grew into months, I realized that this inspiring man of music was completely changing my approach not only to guitar playing but to teaching as well. I was almost disbelieving when he told me we should write a book together, but after he convinced me he wasn't kidding we began work on the book that would become *Beginning Fingerstyle Blues Guitar* (New York: Amsco Publications, 1993). That book has now sold close to 50,000 copies.

My experience with Arnie has been the same, I'm sure, as countless other musicians before me. His teaching is to the point—systematic and effective. His writing style reflects his personality, which is warm, matter-of-fact and full of humor and love for music. His books and explanations proceed in a step-by-step manner serving to illuminate rather than confuse the process. You might think this would be the norm—it turns out it isn't. Arnie is that rare teacher who sees the process from the student's point of view rather than the master's.

In your hands you hold a book that demystifies one of the great guitar styles—*chord melody*. You do not have to be a jazz guitar player to succeed with this book, or even intend to be one. The approach Arnie has mapped out is practical and works for any style of music. I learned so much from participating in the process of writing this book and, once again, felt the excitement of a master teacher gently removing the obstacles to my learning. Good luck and enjoy.

Mark Galbo
Telluride, Colorado

Purpose

The purpose of this book is to teach you to play the melody and chords of a song at the same time, so that the guitar can be performed as a solo instrument and not play only chords or melodies separately. This is the reason the book is called *Beginning Solo Guitar*. A good solo player (such as the great Tony Mottola, or Bucky Pizzarelli, or Al Caiola) can fill a room with music and consequently work many gigs solo that other players cannot. As such, it is a very practical and rewarding style to play. This style is commonly known as "chord melody" guitar and, although it can be used in any style of music, it is generally known as a jazz guitar style. This style of playing was prevalent during the heyday of jazz in the thirties and forties.

In 1959, popular taste in music in this country began to change from what it had been to what it would become. With the change in musical style also came a change in the way the guitar was played.

Groups like the Kingston Trio and Peter, Paul, and Mary swept up the charts with hit songs like "Blowin' In The Wind" and "Tom Dooley." Bob Dylan, accompanying himself on guitar, became known as the poet of his generation and forever changed the course of American music. Then the Beatles came over from England, and with them the "British Invasion." Group after group came to America and their recordings rose to the top of the charts. Folk and rock 'n' roll took over. During this time, thousands of young people all over the world picked up the guitar and made it the most popular instrument of any musical era.

It took awhile to come to understand that the guitar was now being divided into two ways of sounding or playing, either "rhythm" guitar or "lead" guitar. The rhythm guitarist played the guitar as an accompanying instrument, while the lead guitar player played melody. The art of solo guitar was mostly forgotten.

Arnie Berle
New York

Before we begin our study of solo guitar, it is important that we review some things about the chords that we will be using to play our solos. Although you may know a lot of chord fingerings (or chord *forms* or *shapes*), I want to show you some things you may not know.

 TRACK 1 Tuning Notes

Building Chords

All chords come out of scales. For example, the *major* chord comes out of the *major* scale. Below we see a C major scale, and we can see that the C major chord comes from taking the 1st, 3rd, and 5th notes (or *scale degrees*) from the C major scale, and that those notes placed one on top of each other form the C major chord, or C major triad. A *triad* is a chord made up of only three notes.

TRACK 2

C Major Scale

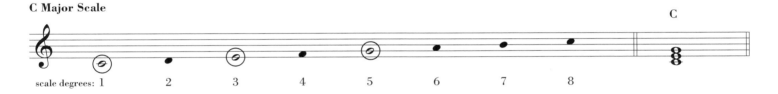

scale degrees: 1   2   3   4   5   6   7   8

Within every major scale there are six additional scales called *modes*. It is from these modes that we form other chords. (The major scale is also known as the *Ionian* mode.) For example, if we start a new scale or mode starting from the second note of the major scale and play up to the same note an octave higher, we create the *Dorian* mode. It is from this mode that we form our *minor* chord.

Below is the D Dorian mode (D being the second note of the C major scale). By taking the 1st, 3rd, and 5th notes from the D Dorian mode, we form the D minor chord (whose chord symbol is **m**). You must remember that when forming the modes that come out of the major scale, the key signature of each mode is the same as the key signature of the original scale. So, the key signature of the D Dorian mode is the same as the key signature of the C major scale.

 TRACK 3

D Dorian Mode

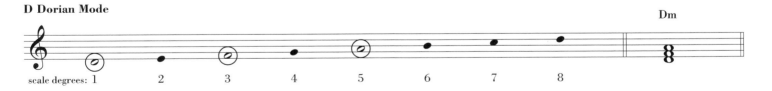

scale degrees: 1   2   3   4   5   6   7   8

10 Chord Review

Now let us look at the next important chord in the scale, which comes from the *Mixolydian* mode. The Mixolydian mode is formed by starting on the fifth note of the original scale and playing up one octave. The Mixolydian mode produces the *dominant 7th* chord. This is a very important chord, which we will see often as we go through the book.

From this mode we take the 1st, 3rd, 5th, and 7th notes and, by placing the notes one on top of each other, we have the dominant 7th chord. The dominant 7th chord, whose chord symbol is simply 7, must have four notes in it. Here is the Mixolydian mode derived from the C major scale. The fifth note of the C scale is the note G, so we will form the G Mixolydian mode.

TRACK 4

G Mixolydian Mode

scale degrees: 1   2   3   4   5   6   7   8

Let us look now at our original C scale and see how the important chords are listed. Notice that beneath each chord are the roman numerals I, II, and V. These roman numerals are used to indicate the numbered position of each chord in the original scale.

TRACK 5

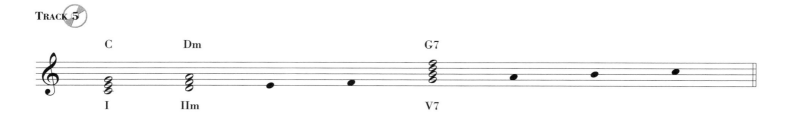

In order to make sure you understand what you've just learned, let us look at two more scales (or keys) and the chords derived from their modes. We start with the F major scale and the F chord:

TRACK 6

F Major Scale

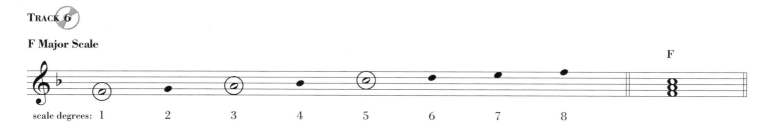

scale degrees: 1   2   3   4   5   6   7   8

Now let's look at the G Dorian mode and the Gm chord:

Track 7

G Dorian Mode

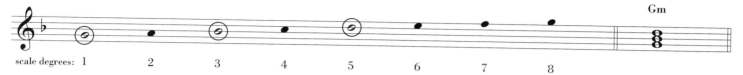

scale degrees: 1   2   3   4   5   6   7   8

Here is the C Mixolydian mode and the C7 chord. Note that the C7 has a B♭ in it because the original scale of F has a B♭ in its key signature.

Track 8

C Mixolydian Mode

scale degrees: 1   2   3   4   5   6   7   8

Here is the F scale with the three chords (I, IIm, and V7) formed from that scale:

Track 9

Chord Review

Let's look at one more scale. Here is the G major scale and the G chord:

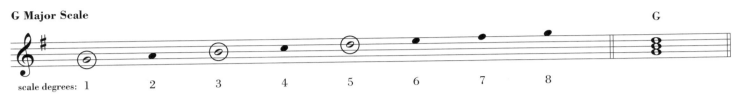

Now let's look at the A Dorian mode and its chord, Am:

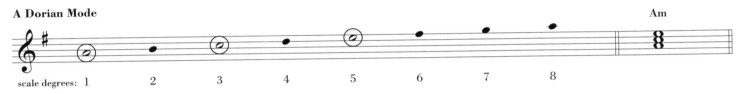

Here is the D Mixolydian mode and the D7 chord. Again, remember that there is an F♯ in our original scale/key and therefore the D7 chord has an F♯ in it.

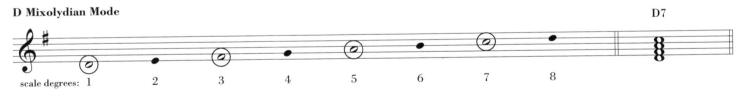

Finally, here is the original G scale with its three most important chords, the I, IIm, and V7.

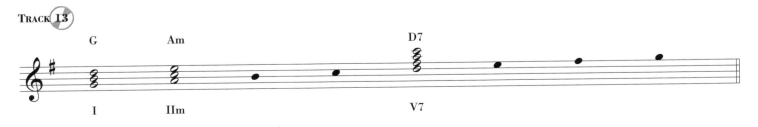

Chord Functions

We have just seen how we form the most important chords from three different scales or keys (the C, F, and G scales). It is also important to know that there are other chords that come out of the other modes that are in the original scale. These other modes are the *Phrygian* mode, which produces the IIIm (minor) chord; the *Lydian* mode, which produces the IV (major) chord; the *Aeolian* mode, which produces the VIm (minor) chord; and the *Locrian* mode, which produces the VII° (diminished) chord. All of these other chords produce three-note chords. The only chord that we learned so far which produces a four-note chord is the V7 chord. The three-note chords will also be extended to four-note chords, which we will see later in the book.

Different chords within a given key perform different *harmonic functions*. Harmony essentially works with *tension* and *release*. Therefore, some chords feel at rest while others have a feeling of motion or create tension.

The I chord is the most important chord in any scale—it is the chord that usually starts a song, and it almost always brings a song to a close. It is a chord of rest. The V7 chord is the second most important chord because it almost always comes just before the I chord, and it is the 7th in that chord which creates the tension that calls for the release in the I chord. The IIm chord, in most cases, sets up or prepares the V7 chord just before the V7 resolves to the I chord. A very popular progression is the famous "two–five–one" (IIm–V7–I), as in Dm–G7–C in the key of C.

The chords from the other modes function as follows:

- The IIIm chord is often used as a substitute for the I chord.
- The IV chord is a major chord like the I chord, and is sometimes used as a substitute for the IIm chord.
- The VIm chord is another minor chord, and sometimes acts as a substitute for the I chord.
- The VII° (the symbol ° is used for diminished chords) chord is sometimes used as a substitute for the V7 chord.

Chord Review

Chord Inversions

An *inverted* chord is a chord in which the order of the notes is changed. For example, in a C chord (C–E–G), the C is placed on the bottom of the chord. The C is the *root* of the chord and the chord is said to be in the *root position*.

However, if the order of notes is changed so that the 3rd is in the bass, as in E–G–C, the chord is said to be in the *first inversion*. If the 5th is left in the bass (G–C–E), the chord is said to be in the *second inversion*.

TRACK 14

Root Position

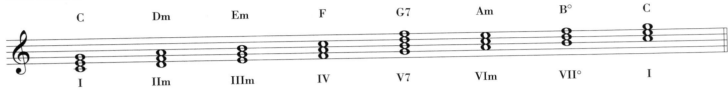

TRACK 15

First Inversion

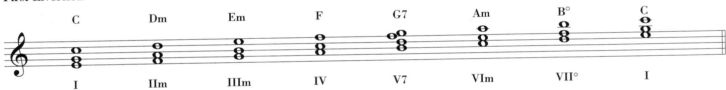

TRACK 16

Second Inversion

When playing rhythm guitar you are usually concentrating on the bass line, but when playing solos on the guitar you must be conscious of the first and second strings because that is where the notes of the melody are best heard.

We will now learn the fingerings for our chords with the roots, 3rds, 5ths, and 7ths (third inversion) on the first string. Begin with the F major triad and play the root position, first inversion, and second inversion. Then go back and transpose to F♯ and continue up the neck in all twelve keys.

Major Triads

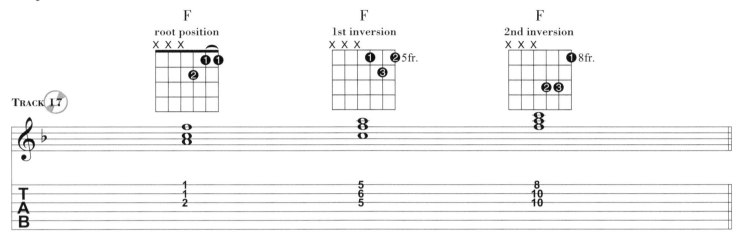

Minor Triads

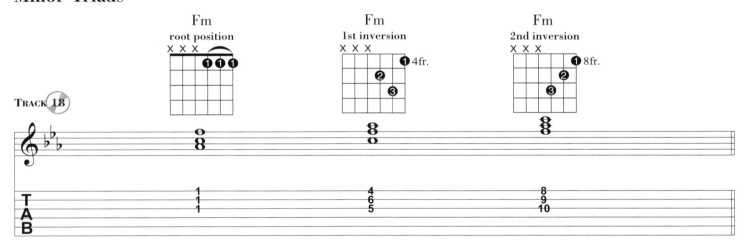

Dominant 7ths

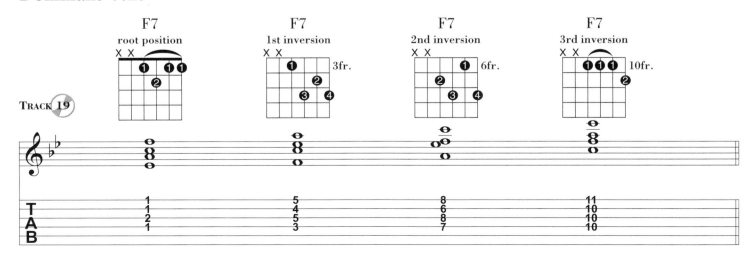

Melody on the First String

Frère Jacques

The tune we are going to play is a familiar and traditional melody. We see that the song is written in the key of F. The two most important chords are used in this tune—the I (F) and the V7 (C7).

Here is the tune in its original form. As we look at the tune for the first time, we find that it is written very low on the guitar fingerboard. Obviously, it can be played in this position, but not with the chords as a solo on the guitar.

Here is the tune raised an octave. Now it is playable with chords.

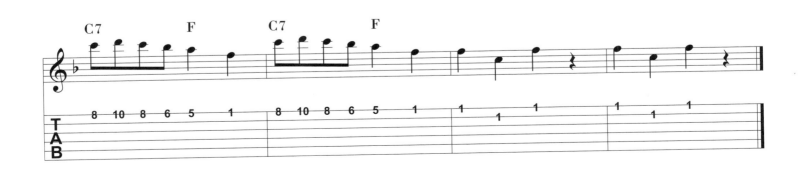

The note F is played on the first beat of measures 1, 2, 7, and 8. Since F is the root of the F chord, you must play the root-position chord on the first beat of those measures. In measures 3 and 4, you must play the F chord with the 3rd (A) on the top string, and then with the 5th (C) on top.

In the fifth and sixth measures, the chord to be played is the C7 in the root position. Remember that all of the melody notes are to be played on the first string.

FRÈRE JACQUES IN F (CHORD SOLO)

Melody on the Second String

The following diagrams show the major, minor, and dominant chords with the root, 3rd, 5th, and 7th on the second string. We will start with the D major chord, whose root is on the third fret.

Major Triads

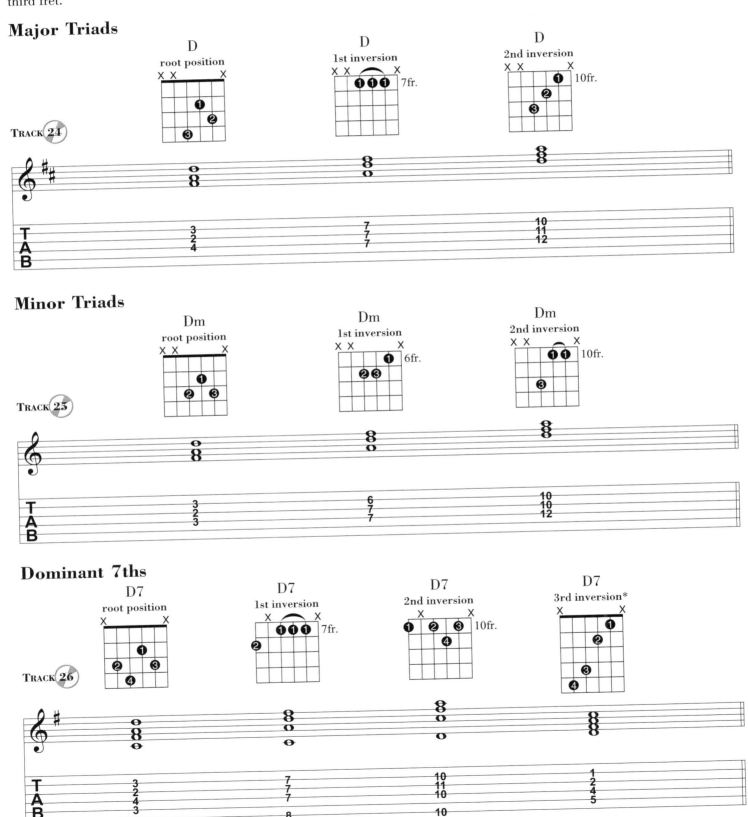

Minor Triads

Dominant 7ths

* Notice that the dominant 7th chord with the 7th on the second string could be rather difficult to play up on the thirteenth fret (it would be better to play this D7 with the 7th on the first string). The diagram above shows the D7 down an octave, with the 7th on the first fret. You can use it there or try playing it up on the higher frets.

Let's play "Frère Jacques" in the key of D major using a second-string melody. The I chord is D and the V7 chord is A7.

FRÈRE JACQUES IN D (CHORD SOLO)

TRACKS 27 & 28

Melody on Two Strings

"Red River Valley" is in the key of G but, in the second measure, the G becomes a G7, which means that it has become the dominant (V7) chord of the temporary key of C. The tune goes directly back to the key of G and ends with the I–IV–I ending (G–C–G).

In the second measure, the melody note is A, but the chord is still G7 (A is not in our G7 chord). To harmonize the note A with the G7 chord, play the G7 chord with the G melody note on the first string and simply add an A at the fifth fret, first string.

RED RIVER VALLEY

TRACKS 29 & 30

"Amazing Grace" is similar to "Red River Valley." We start with a V-chord pickup to the key of G, and then use the temporary dominant G7 to move to C. In measure 6, we use another temporary dominant (A7) to set up the D chord, which immediately becomes D7 to lead us back to G.

At the end of each phrase, the melody note is held while the chords change underneath. Since this tune is very well known, the melody will stay in the listener's ear, leaving you free to change chords normally. You will use this trick in almost every chord solo you play.

AMAZING GRACE

Major 7th and Minor 7th Chords

Major 7th Chords on the First String

We learned that the dominant 7th chord is formed by taking the 1st, 3rd, 5th, and 7th notes from the Mixolydian mode. The major 7th (**maj7**) chord is formed by taking the 1st, 3rd, 5th, and 7th notes from the major scale:

TRACK 31

The major 7th chord is just another I chord, since it is built on the first note of the major scale. Here are the Fmaj7 chords on the first string, starting at the first fret:

TRACK 32

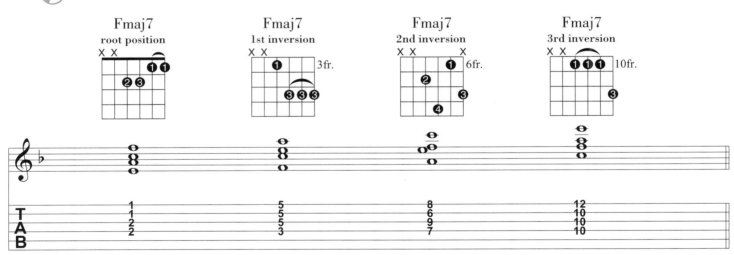

Minor 7th Chords on the First String

Although there are three different modes that can produce a minor chord, we are going to stick with the Dorian mode. You have already learned that taking the 1st, 3rd, and 5th notes from the Dorian mode forms a minor chord. So, to form the minor 7th (**m7**) chord, we will now take the 1st, 3rd, 5th, and 7th notes of the Dorian mode.

TRACK 33

D Dorian Mode

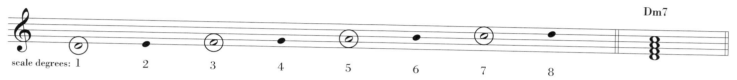

We are now going to learn the fingerings for the minor 7th chord and all its inversions on the first string. We will use Fm7 simply because it can start on the first fret. Remember that although we are starting on Fm7, this chord comes from the F Dorian mode and that the original (major) scale is E♭.

TRACK 34

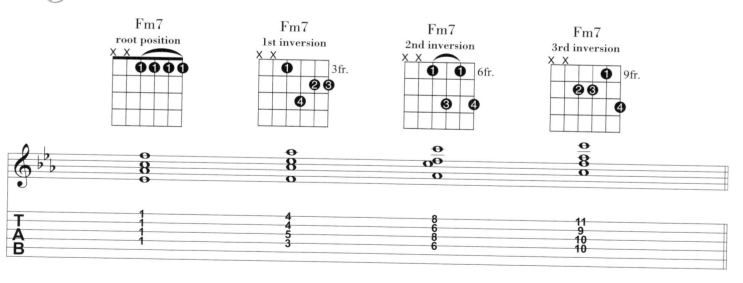

Major 7th and Minor 7th Chords

"Aura Lee" was a very popular song during the days of the Civil War, written here in the key of G. It was sung both by the Union and Confederate soldiers alike. While it is true that in these original folk tunes it was common to use simple or unadorned chords, in this case I have extended the chords to include major and minor 7ths. Adding 7ths makes the chords sound more modern.

Play the song twice, once with the 7ths added and once again with simple triads (without the added 7ths). You can decide which you prefer. In the first measure we play the Gmaj7 with the 5th on the second string (see page 26). Notice that after the fourth measure there is a *repeat sign* (:‖), which tells the player to go back to the beginning and play those measures once again. The repeat sign is a way of saving space.

AURA LEE

"Earth Angel" is a tune built on a progression that has been used for hundreds of songs since the 1920s, in every field of music from pop to jazz to rock and roll. The progression is I–VIm–IIm–V7, and in this tune (in the key of G major) that progression would be G–Em–Am–D7. Originally, this tune was written in E♭, but it is a little easier to play in the key of G.

Notice that on the third beat in the second measure, the melody note is a B. Play the D7 with the C melody note on top and just move your finger one fret lower from the C to the B, sounding out a B melody above the D7 chord. Notice also that in the seventh and eighth measures the melody note is just a G, and that I put in the I–IIm7–V chords (G–Am7–D). I left out the VIm chord so that I can go directly to the I chord (G), which brings the tune to a rest at the end.

EARTH ANGEL (WILL YOU BE MINE)

Track 36

Words and Music by Jesse Belvin

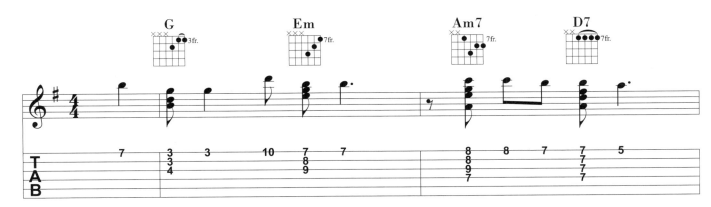

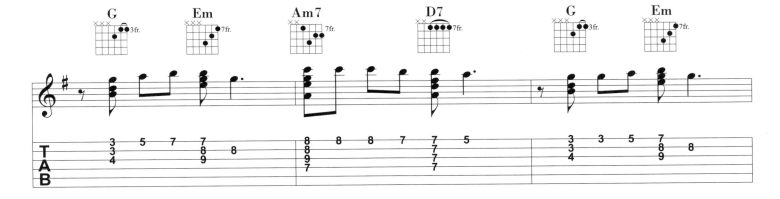

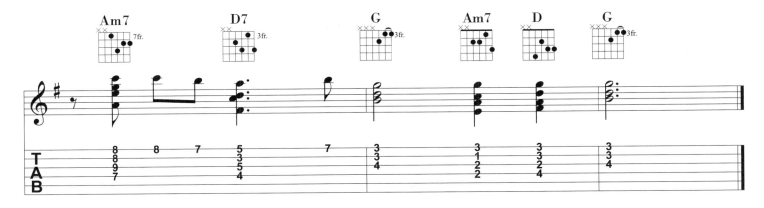

Major 7th Chords on the Second String

Now we will learn how to play major 7th chords with the melody note on the second string. Below are the fingerings for all the inversions of the Dmaj7 chord.

TRACK 37

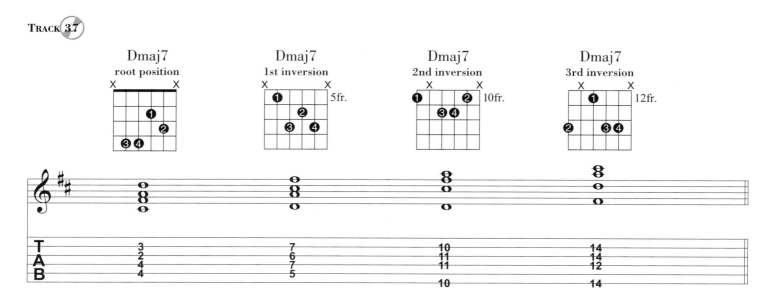

It might be easier to think of the note D as the root of the Dmaj7, then as the 3rd of the Bbmaj7, the 5th of the Gmaj7, and then finally as the 7th of the Ebmaj7. Playing these different forms in this way might be easier to see because all of the shapes are in the same position on the fingerboard.

For example, if you need a Dmaj7 with the 7th on the second string, you would think of the D as the major 7th of Ebmaj7 and then raise your hand up to the C♯ (the major 7th of Dmaj7) on the second string and then finger the chord as if you were playing the Ebmaj7.

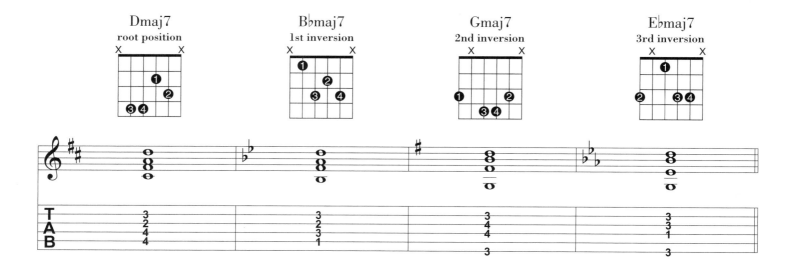

Minor 7th Chords on the Second String

We will now play the minor 7th chords with the melody on the second string. The minor 7th chord may be thought of as a IIm chord, a IIIm chord, or a VIm chord depending on its usage. However, the fingerings for all the minor 7ths are the same.

 TRACK 38

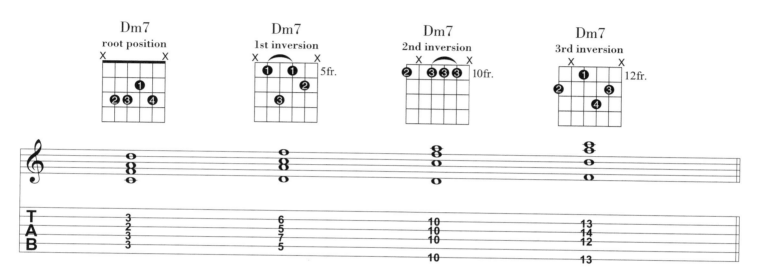

Try the same exercise that you did with the major 7th chords. Think of D as the root of Dm7, then as the 3rd of Bm7, the 5th of Gm7, and finally, as the 7th of Em7. It may be easier to see these chords around the third and fourth frets, and then move your hand to the correct inversion of whatever chords you are working on.

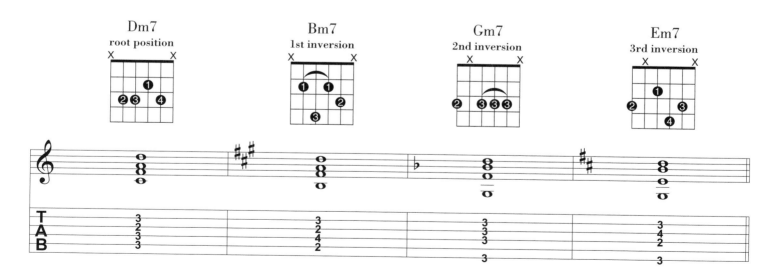

Major 7th and Minor 7th Chords

"Londonderry Air" is a very beautiful Irish song also known as "Danny Boy." Although the chords in this song are basically simple Gs, Cs, and Fs, I thought you might like to try some more extended chords and so I gave you a lot of major 6th chords (chord symbol 6).

The 6th note is just one note above the 5th of the chord, so G6 is G–B–D–E, F6 is F–A–C–D, and C6 is C–E–G–A. I am going to let you find the 6ths when you play these chords. The tune may also be played without the added 6ths, playing just the straight G, C, and F chords.

LONDONDERRY AIR

TRACK 39

Every major scale or key has a *relative minor* scale or key. The keys are said to be "related" because they share the same key signature. The relative minor can be found starting on the sixth note of the major scale. For example, in the key of C major (no sharps or flats), the sixth note of the major scale is the note A, which becomes the first note of the A minor scale (key of A minor).

There are three minor scales. The first one is the scale played from A to A as explained above, and is called the *natural* minor scale. The second minor scale is from A to A again, but you raise the seventh note a *half step* (on guitar, one fret). This is called the *harmonic* minor scale. The third minor scale is built from A to A again, but the sixth and seventh notes are raised a half step going up the scale and lowered going back down. This is called the *melodic* minor scale.

Let's see how the three scales look. Remember that the C major scale and the three A minor scales all share the same key signature.

TRACK 40

A Natural Minor

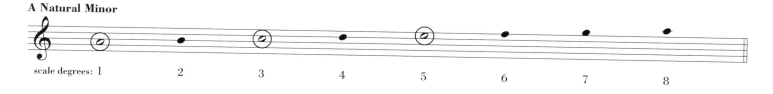

scale degrees: 1   2   3   4   5   6   7   8

TRACK 41

A Harmonic Minor

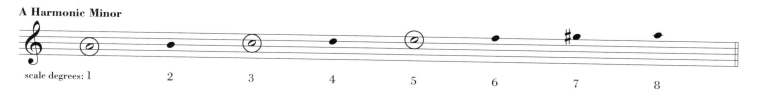

scale degrees: 1   2   3   4   5   6   7   8

TRACK 42

A Melodic Minor

scale degrees: 1 2 3 4 5 6 7 8 7 6 5 4 3 2 1

Minor Keys

Our next song, "Greensleeves," is based on an old waltz and, although it was originally written in the key of A minor, I have put the song into the key of E minor to make it more playable.

You will come to realize that a song written in a minor key tends to sound a bit melancholy, while a song in a major key has a much happier quality.

GREENSLEEVES

TRACK 43

Diminished 7th Chords

"Everything Happens To Me" is a very popular song that jazz singers love to sing. It is written in the key of G, which has one sharp (F♯) in the key signature, but the chords move around from key to key. For example, the first two chords are the IIm–V in G, but instead of resolving to G they go on to another key. Now let's look at some of the other chords. In the first measure there is an Am7 chord with the melody note B. Finger the Am7 chord with the root on top and stretch the pinky up to the note B on the seventh fret.

In the third measure there is a D7 chord, and here is a case where you have to use the open D string. The reason for the open string is that the F♯ played at the second fret doesn't leave enough room to play the note D, so you have no choice but to play the open D string. Of course, you can play the D7 at the seventh fret and that will allow you to play the D on the fifth string. That is a choice you will have to make.

There are also some diminished 7th chords in this piece (chord symbol °7). The diminished 7th chord is a modern sounding chord, and there are two fingerings used here.

The first one (G°7, second measure) has the root on the first string, and the next diminished 7th chord (D°7, fifth measure) has the root on the second string. Here are the two chord fingerings:

Track 44

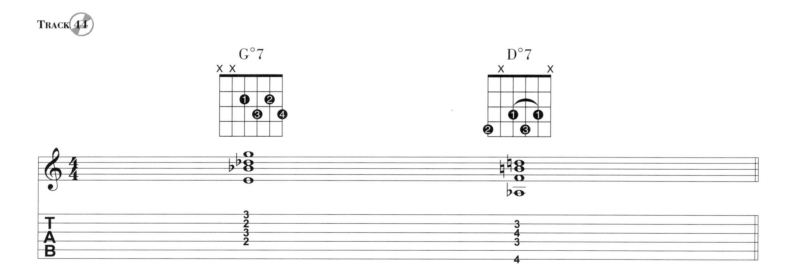

EVERYTHING HAPPENS TO ME

TRACK 45

Words and Music by Matt Dennis and Tom Adair

Creating Your Own Chord Melodies

The following tunes are now given to the student with just the melody and chord symbols (without the chord diagrams or notes of the chords written in). The purpose of this is to see how well you can make your own choices and to see if you have memorized much of what you learned by playing through this book. All the tunes are fairly simple and you should have no trouble.

There are many different options. If you need to, fill in the blank chord frames and notes of the chords in the space provided. The following charts give you the roots, 3rds, 5ths, and 7ths of the three different seventh chords—the major 7th, the minor 7th, and the dominant 7th chords. Memorize all of these notes so that you can use them in your guitar solos.

Major 7ths

Chord Name	Root	3rd	5th	7th
Cmaj7	C	E	G	B
C#maj7	C#	E#	G#	B#
Dbmaj7	Db	F	Ab	C
Dmaj7	D	F#	A	C#
Ebmaj7	Eb	G	Bb	D
Emaj7	E	G#	B	D#
Fmaj7	F	A	C	E
F#maj7	F#	A#	C#	E#
Gmaj7	G	B	D	F#
Abmaj7	Ab	C	Eb	G
Amaj7	A	C#	E	G#
Bbmaj7	Bb	D	F	A
Bmaj7	B	D#	F#	A#

Minor 7ths

Chord Name	Root	3rd	5th	7th
Cm7	C	Eb	G	Bb
C#m7	C#	E	G#	B
Dbm7	Db	Fb	Ab	Cb
Dm7	D	F	A	C
Ebm7	Eb	Gb	Bb	Db
Em7	E	G	B	D
Fm7	F	Ab	C	Eb
F#m7	F#	A	C#	E
Gm7	G	Bb	D	F
Abm7	Ab	Cb	Eb	Gb
Am7	A	C	E	G
Bbm7	Bb	Db	F	Ab
Bm7	B	D	F#	A

Dominant 7ths

Chord Name	Root	3rd	5th	7th
C7	C	E	G	Bb
C#7	C#	E#	G#	B
Db7	Db	F	Ab	Cb
D7	D	F#	A	C
Eb7	Eb	G	Bb	Db
E7	E	G#	B	D
F7	F	A	C	Eb
F#7	F#	A#	C#	E
G7	G	B	D	F
Ab7	Ab	C	Eb	Gb
A7	A	C#	E	G
Bb7	Bb	D	F	Ab
B7	B	D#	F#	A

Below is an illustration showing all the notes up to the twelfth fret on the guitar. You will notice that the fingerboard repeats at the twelfth fret, but an octave higher. Look at the notes on the fingerboard as you are playing to see what notes make up each chord formation. Use this diagram to learn all the note names on each string at each fret.

In the next group of tunes, you will see that there are no fingerings in the chord diagrams. The tablature for each melody is given as a suggestion only, to help you get started. This will be a chance for you to see how much you have learned. You should now be able to play a solo on any tune you wish.

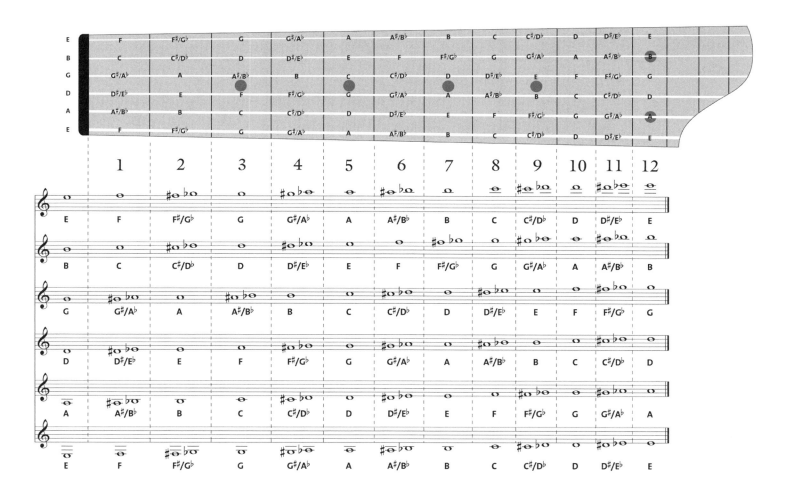

Creating Your Own Chord Melodies

THIS LITTLE LIGHT OF MINE

TRACK 46

All Through The Night

Creating Your Own Chord Melodies

JACOB, DRINK

TRACK 48

AMERICA

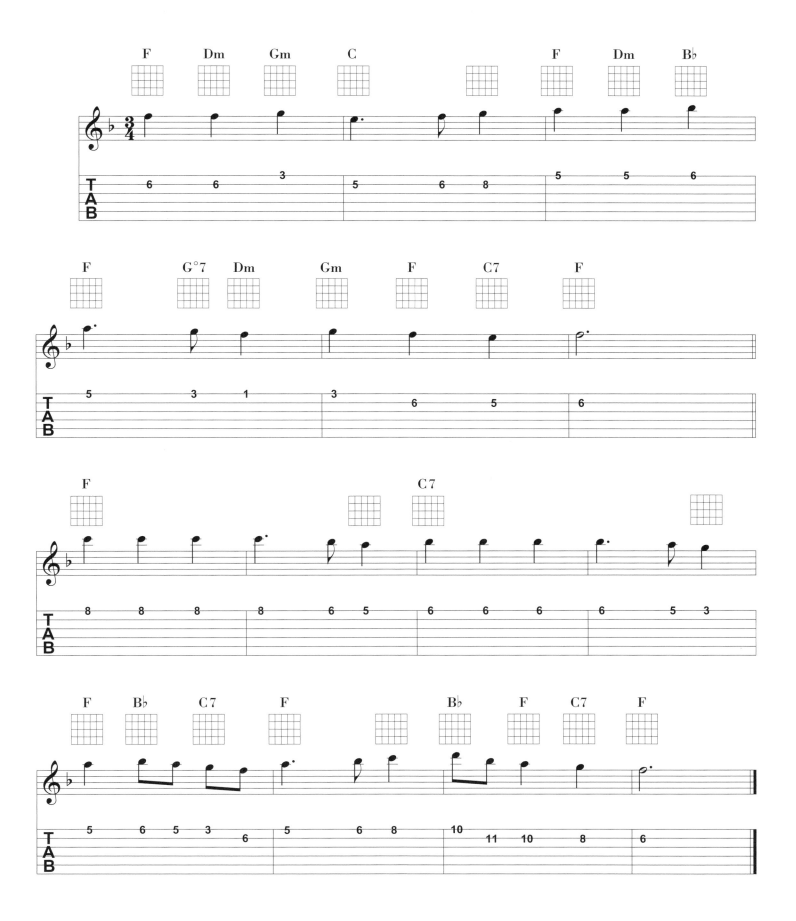

Creating Your Own Chord Melodies

HOME ON THE RANGE

Creating Your Own Chord Melodies

You are given just the chord symbols for "The Star-Spangled Banner." As an exercise, try to harmonize every note of the melody.

Try to play as many different chord solos as possible. Play the melody notes on different strings, use different inversions, and choose different notes to harmonize.

THE STAR-SPANGLED BANNER

Words by Francis Scott Key
Music by John Stafford Smith

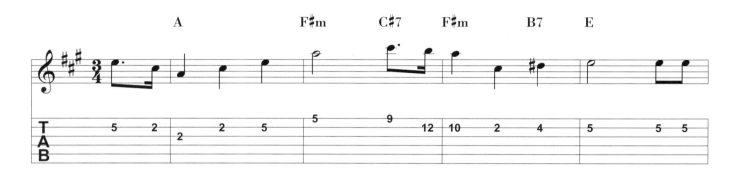

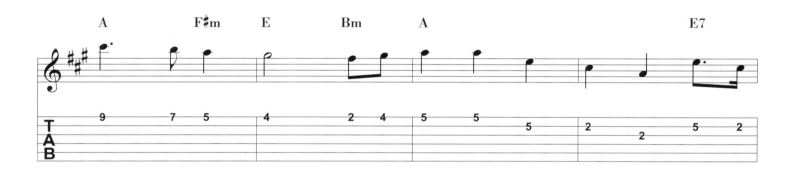

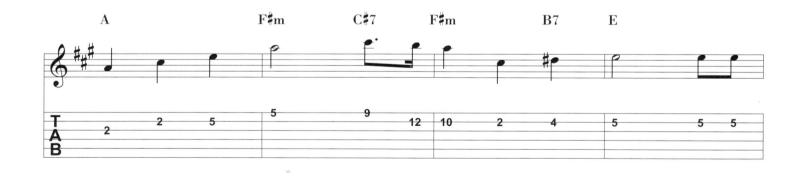

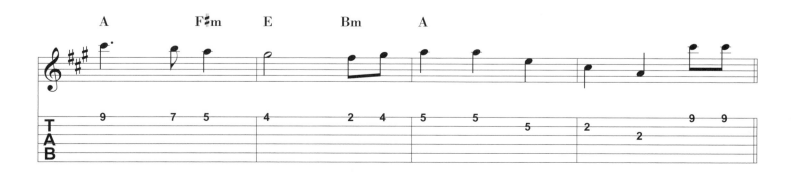

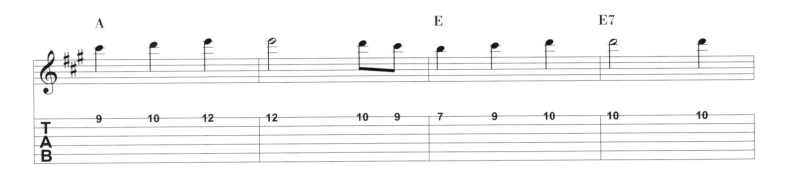

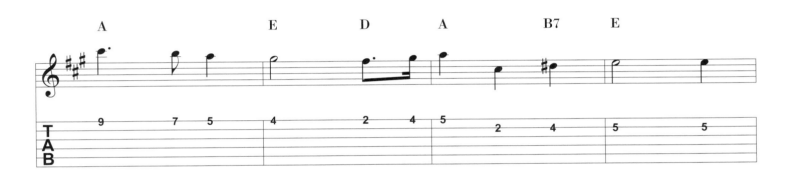

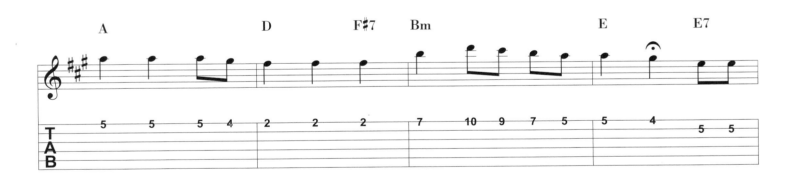

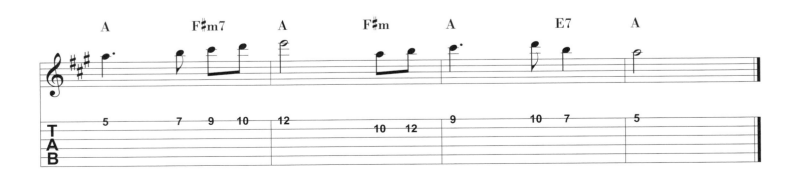

The following chord dictionary has many different chord shapes and inversions for almost any chord symbol you might encounter.

They are shown here in the key of F, but can be transposed to any chord you need by finding the appropriate root and melody note.

F

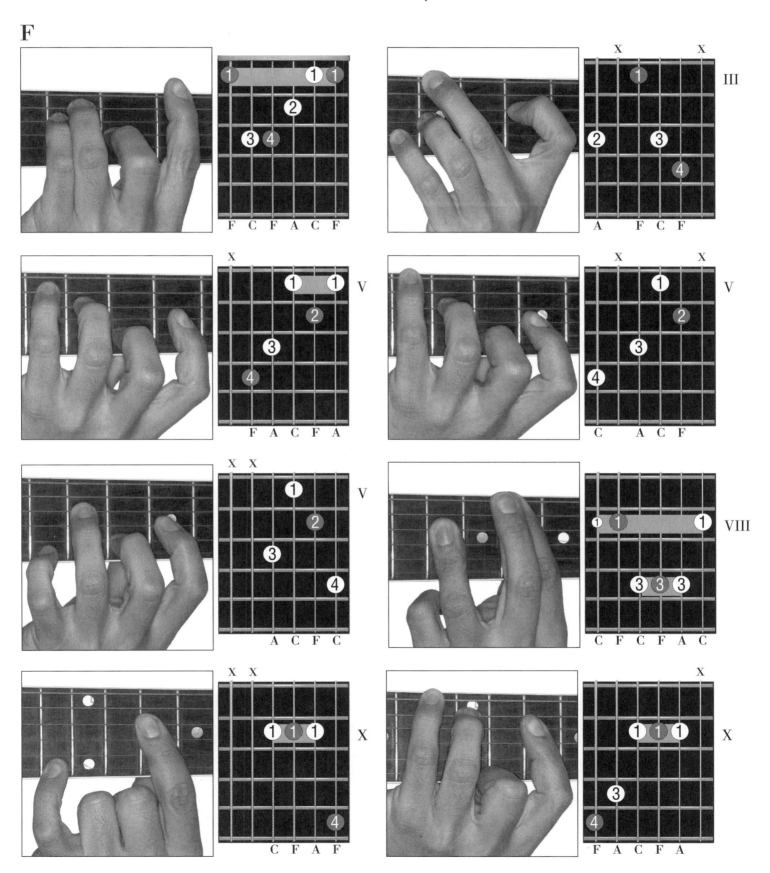

Fsus4

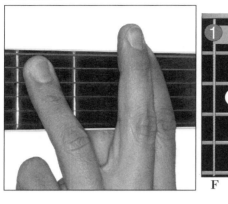
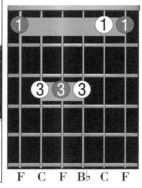

F C F B♭ C F

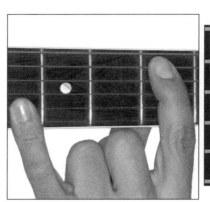
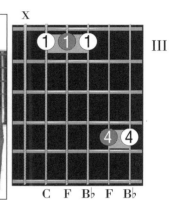

X   III

C F B♭ F B♭

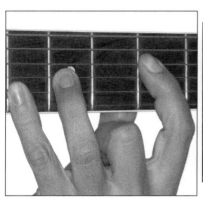
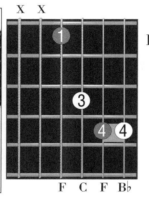

X X   III

F C F B♭

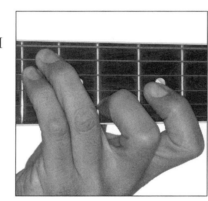
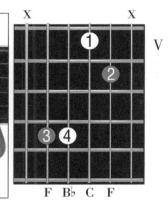

X   X   V

F B♭ C F

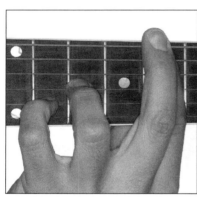
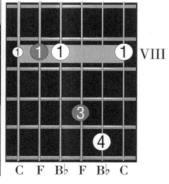

VIII

C F B♭ F B♭ C

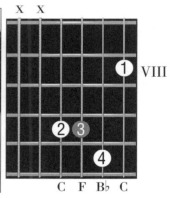

X X   VIII

C F B♭ C

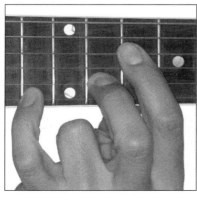
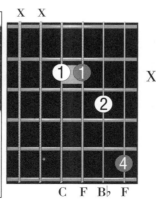

X X   X

C F B♭ F

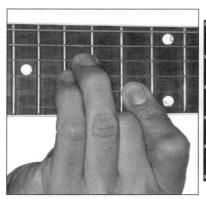
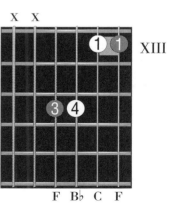

X X   XIII

F B♭ C F

F6

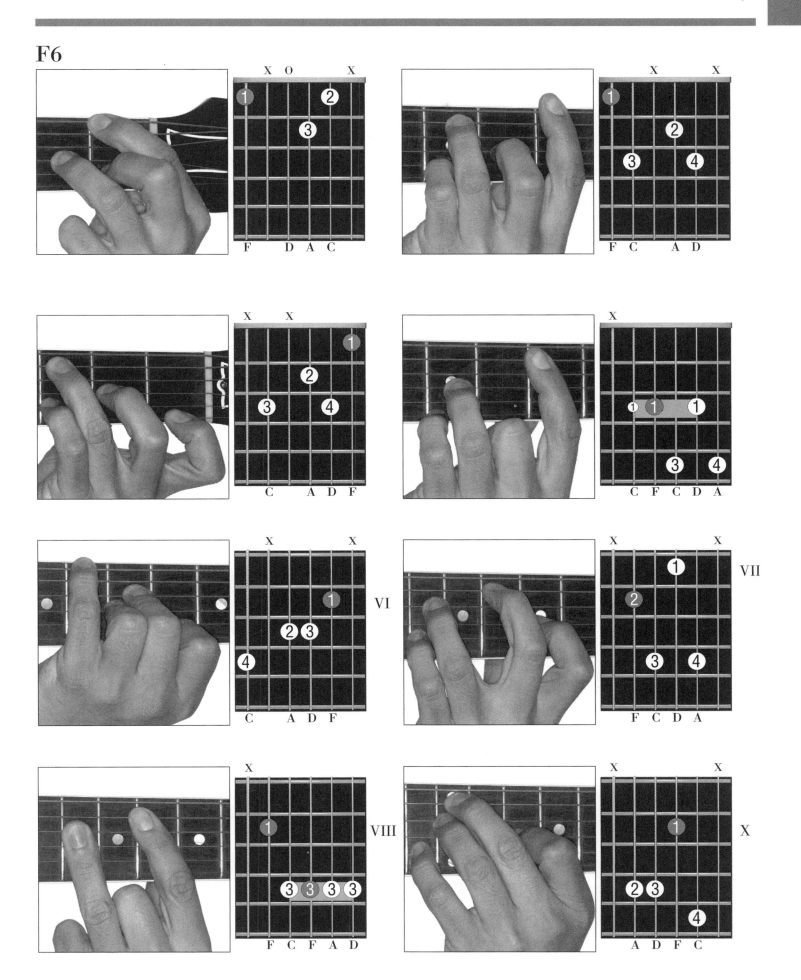

F6/9

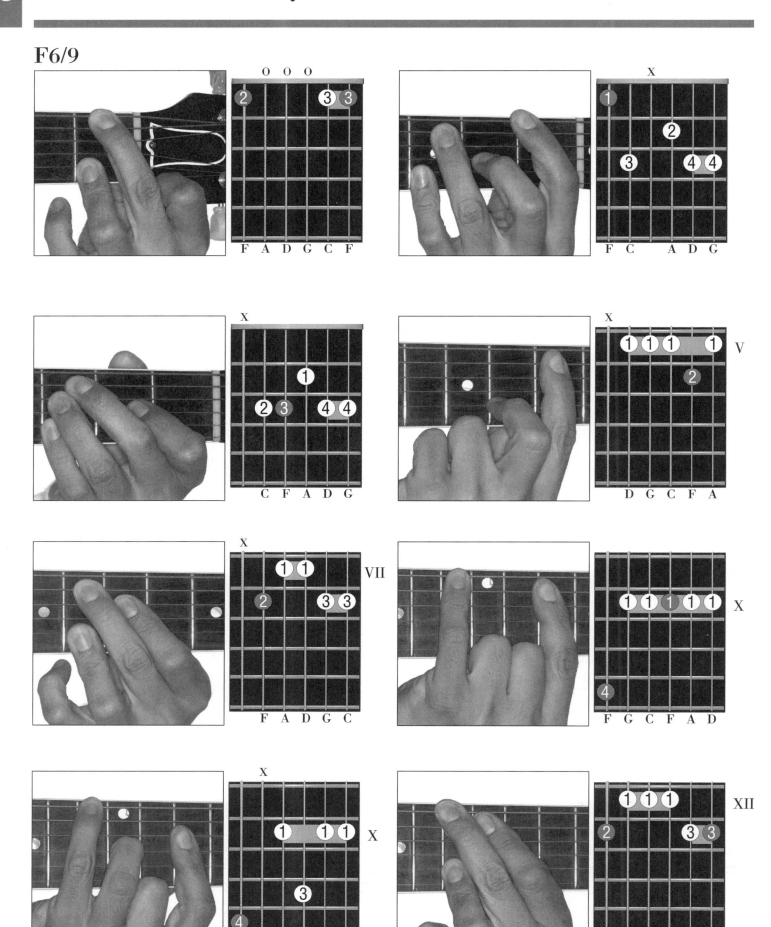

Fmaj7

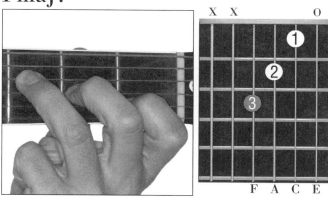

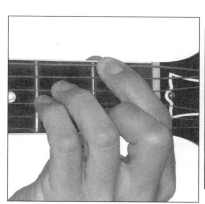

X X   O

F A C E

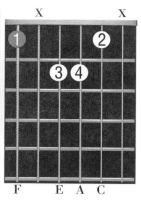

X   X

F   E A C

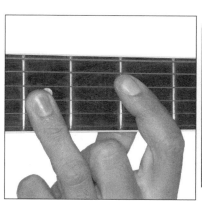

X X

F C E A

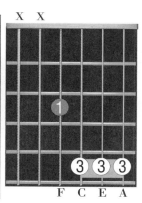

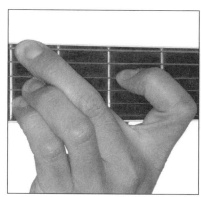

X   X

A   F C E

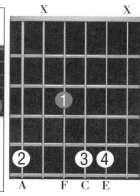

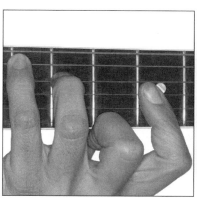

X

F A C E A   V

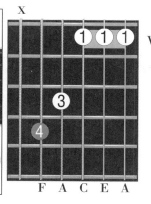

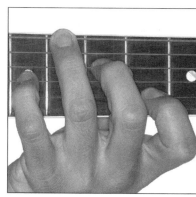

X   X

C   A E F   VI

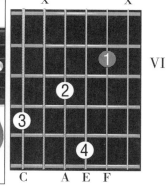

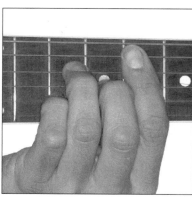

X

F C E A C   VIII

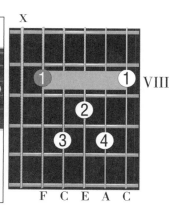

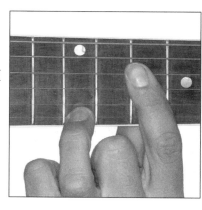

X X

C F A E   X

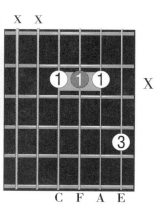

Fmaj9

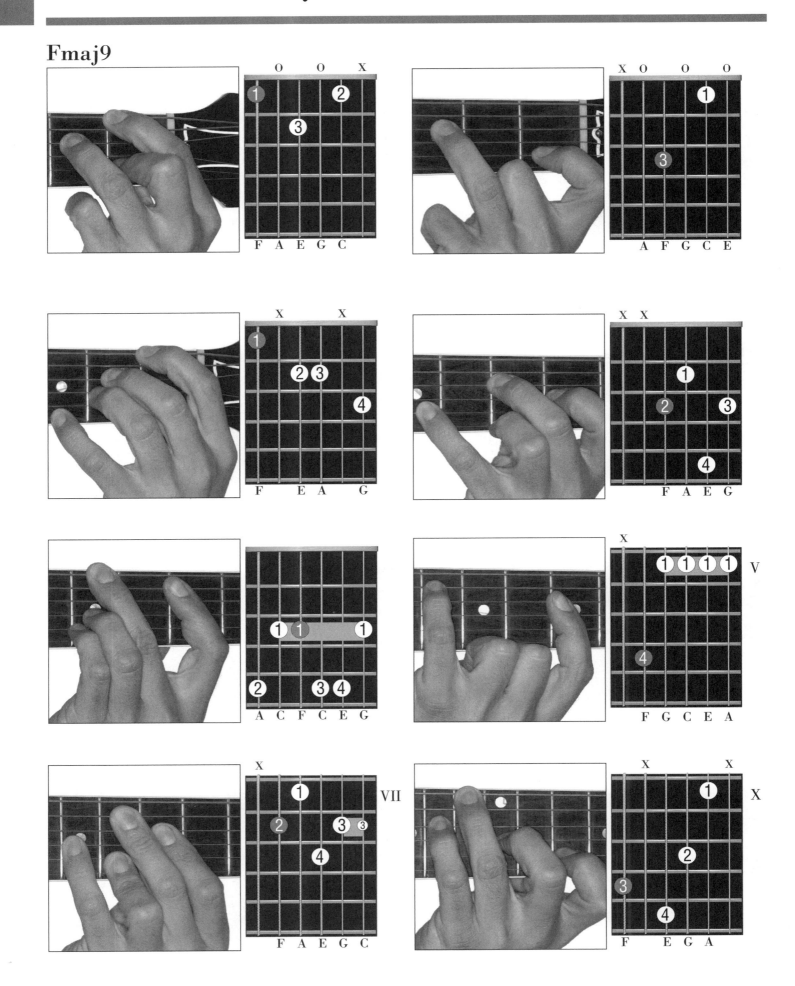

Fm

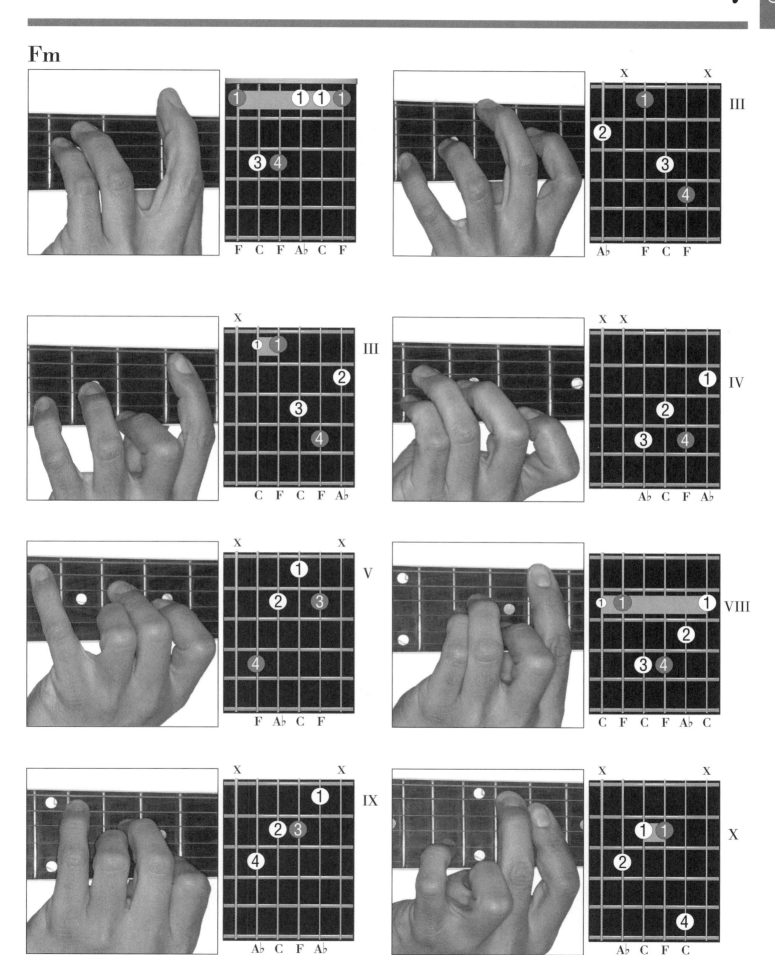

Fm6

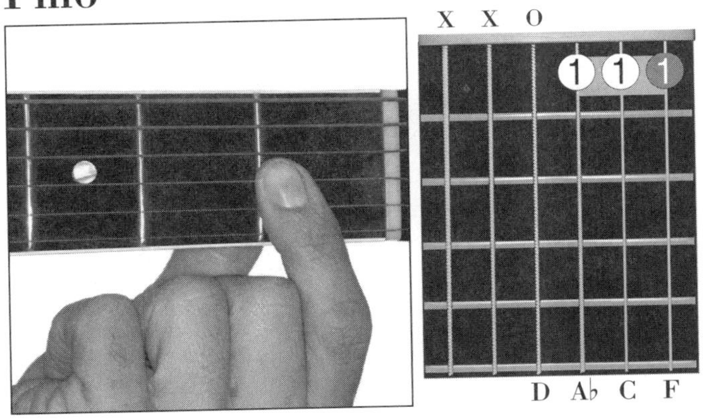

X X O

1 1 1

D A♭ C F

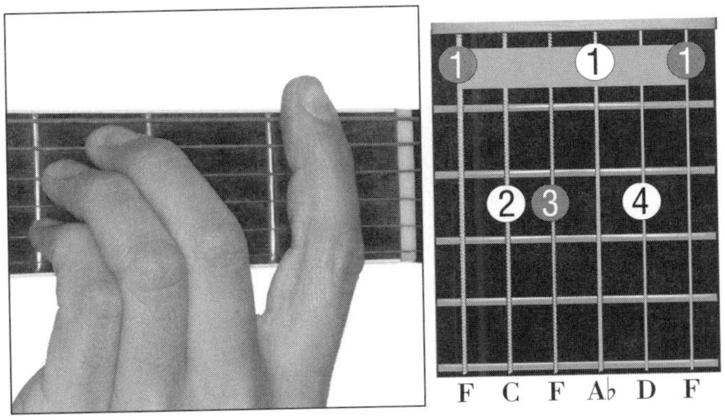

1 1 1

2 3 4

F C F A♭ D F

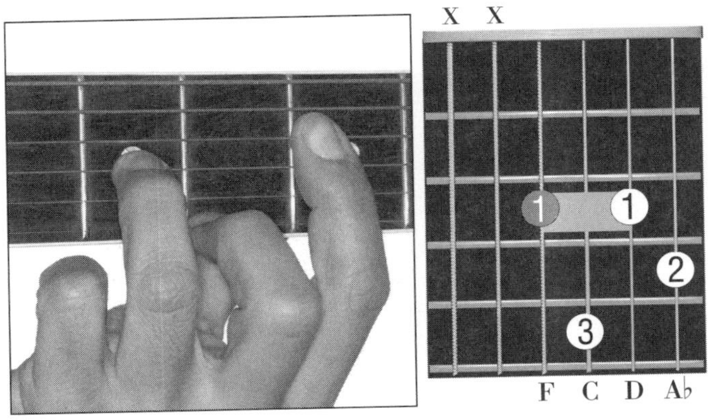

X X

1 1

2

3

F C D A♭

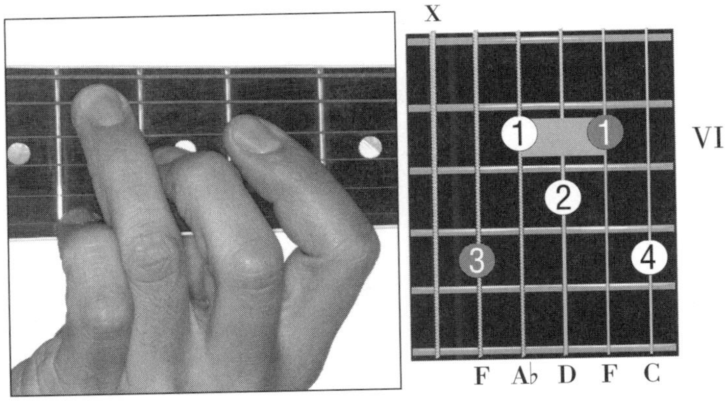

X

1 1 VI

2

3 4

F A♭ D F C

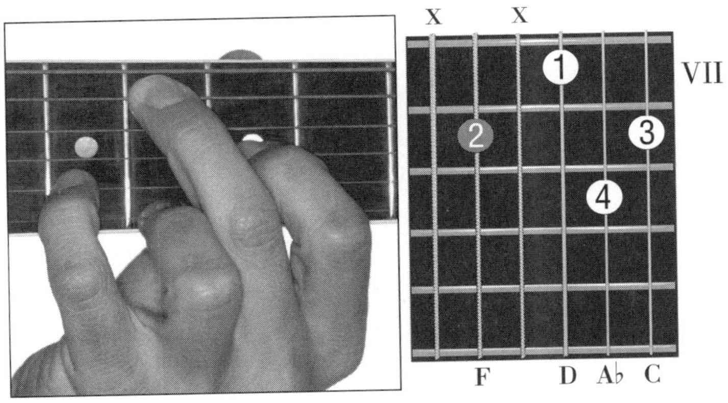

X X

1 VII

2 3

4

F D A♭ C

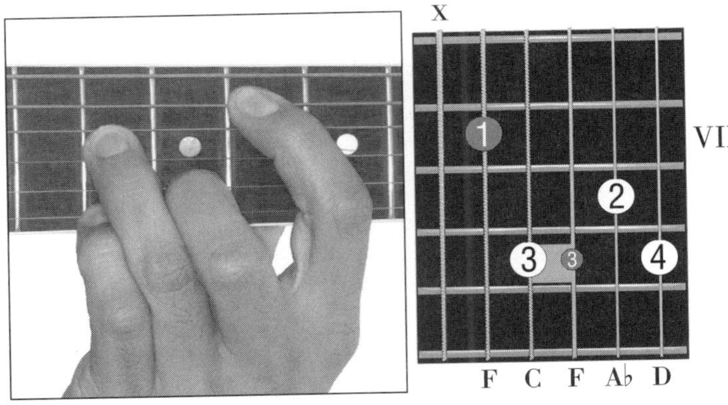

X

1 VIII

2

3 3 4

F C F A♭ D

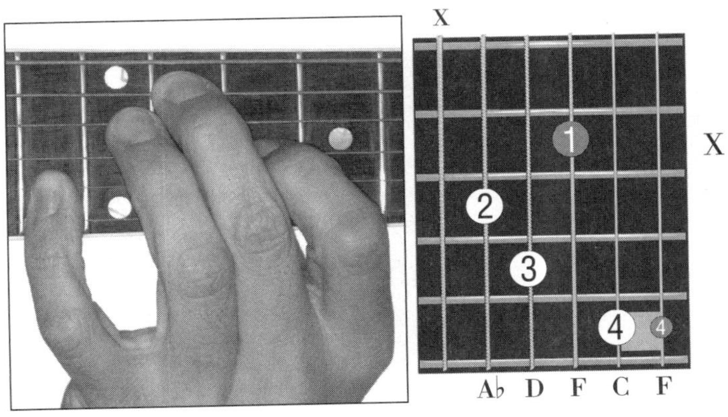

X

1 X

2

3

4 4

A♭ D F C F

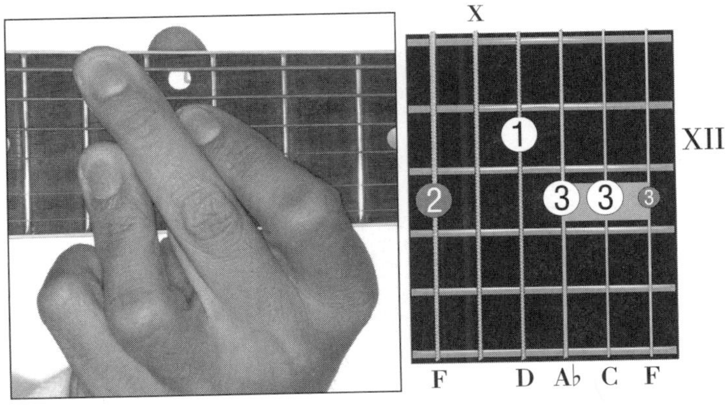

X

1 XII

2 3 3 3

F D A♭ C F

Fm7

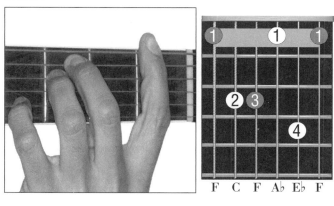

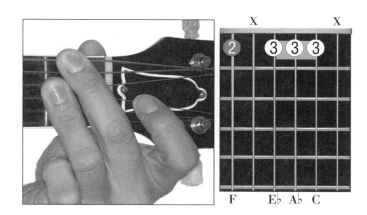

F C F A♭ E♭ F

X   X

F   E♭ A♭ C

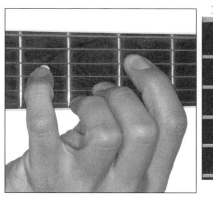

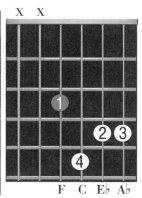

X X

F C E♭ A♭

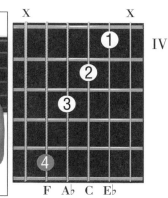

X   X

IV

F A♭ C E♭

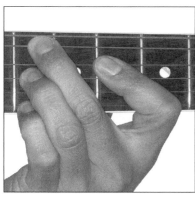

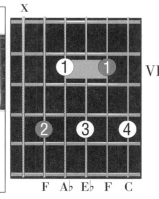

X

VI

F A♭ E♭ F C

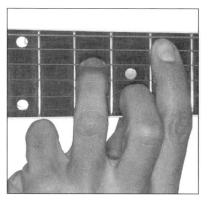

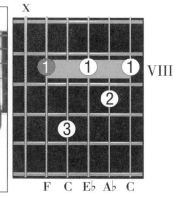

X

VIII

F C E♭ A♭ C

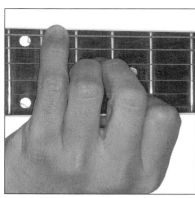

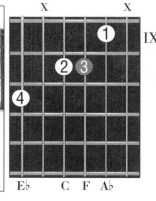

X   X

IX

E♭   C F A♭

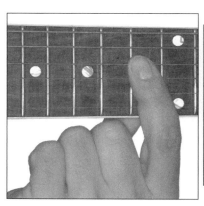

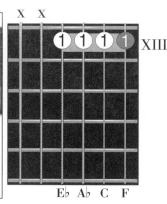

X X

XIII

E♭ A♭ C F

Chord Dictionary

Fm(maj7)

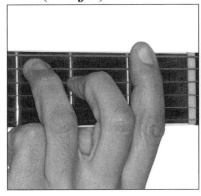
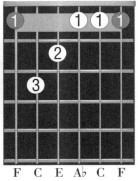
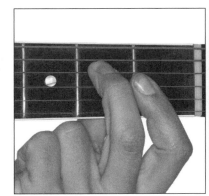
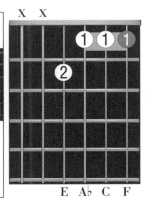

F C E A♭ C F

E A♭ C F

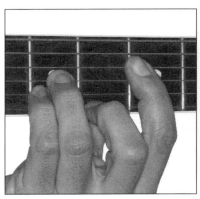
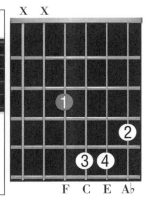
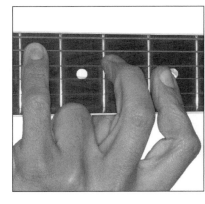
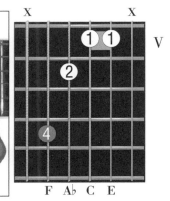

F C E A♭

V

F A♭ C E

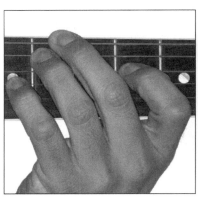
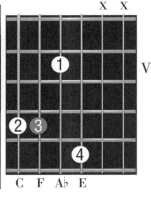

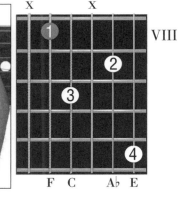

VI

C F A♭ E

VIII

F C A♭ E

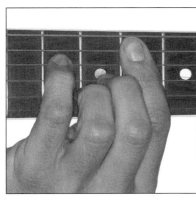
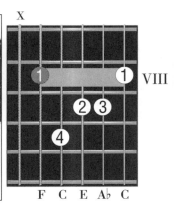

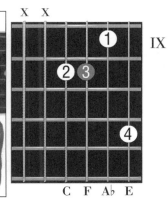

VIII

F C E A♭ C

IX

C F A♭ E

Fm9

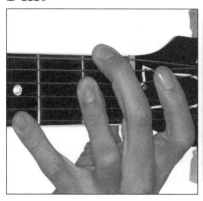

F Eb Ab C G

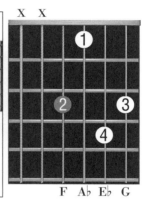

F Ab Eb G

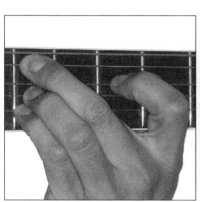
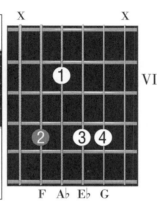

VI

F Ab Eb G

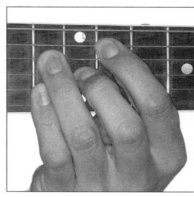
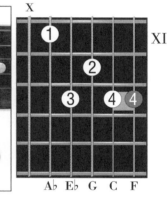

XI

Ab Eb G C F

Fm11

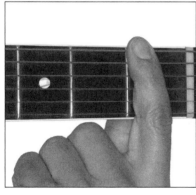
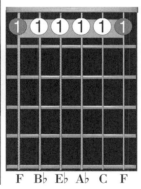

F Bb Eb Ab C F

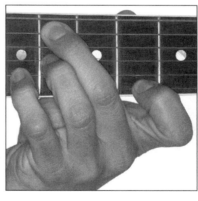
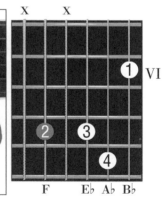

VI

F Eb Ab Bb

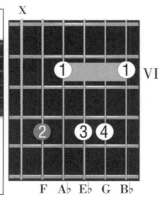

VI

F Ab Eb G Bb

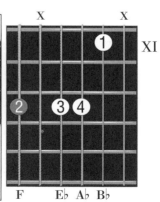

XI

F Eb Ab Bb

Fm7♭5

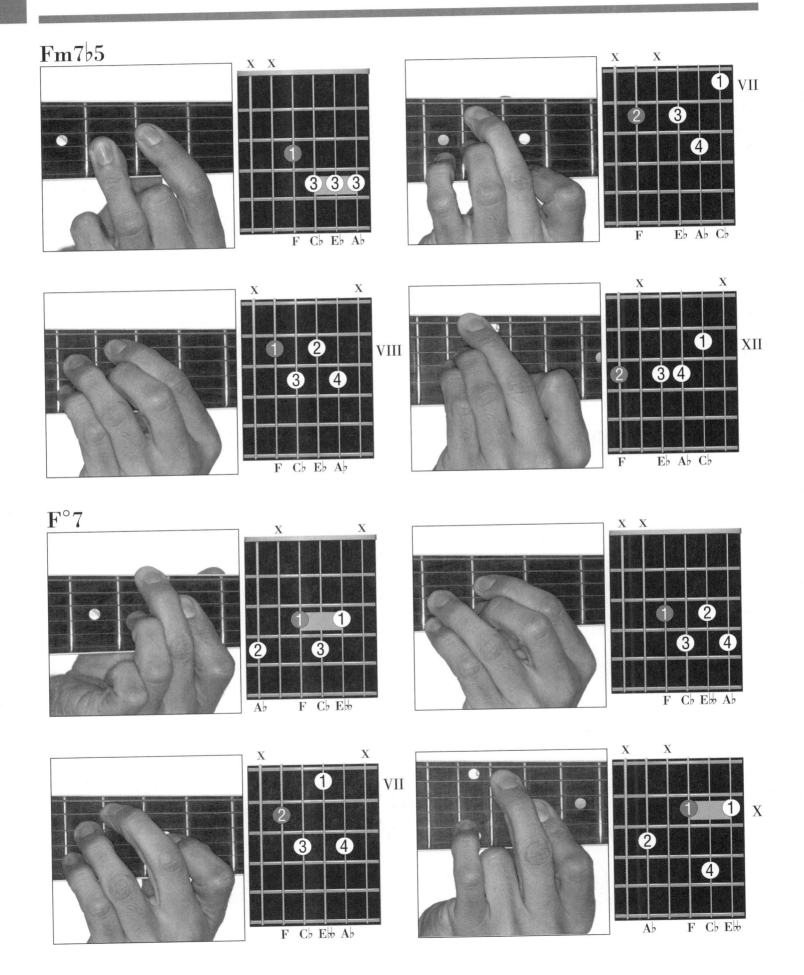

F°7

F7

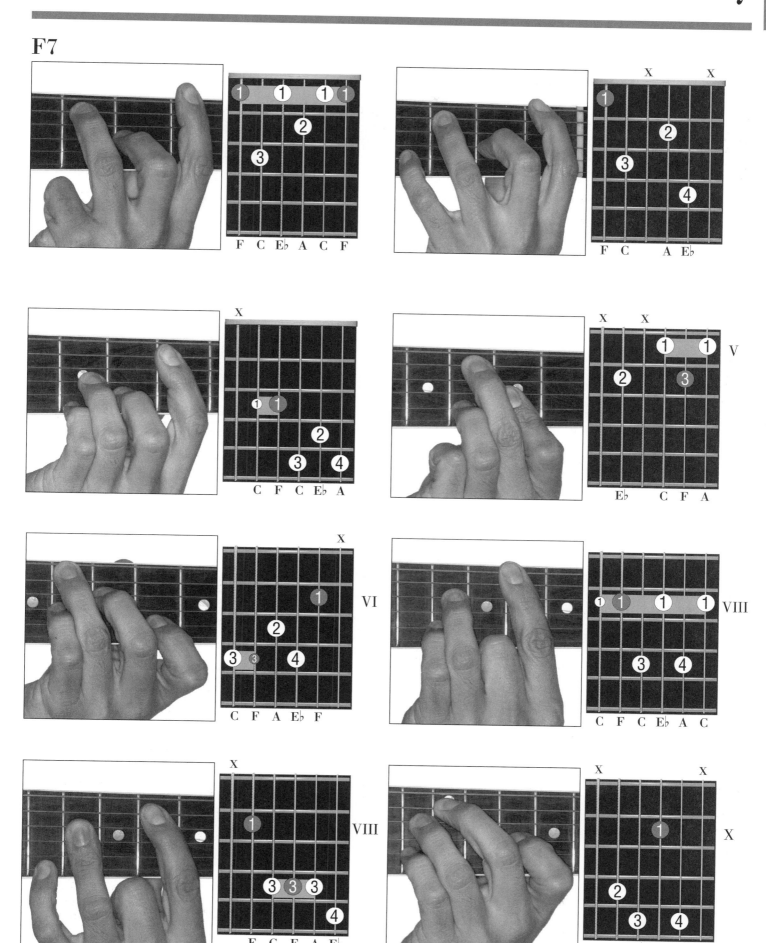

Chord Dictionary

F7sus4

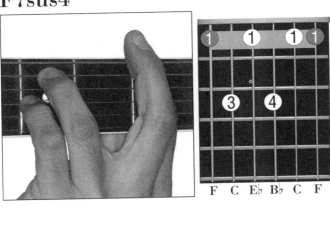
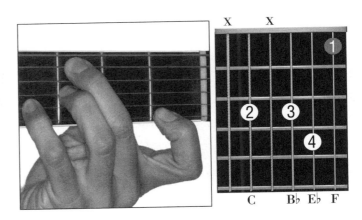

F C E♭ B♭ C F

X X
C B♭ E♭ F

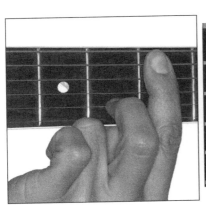 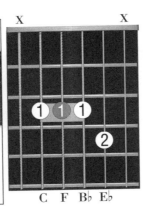
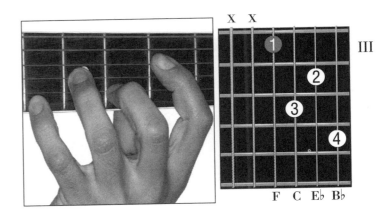

X X
C F B♭ E♭

X X
III
F C E♭ B♭

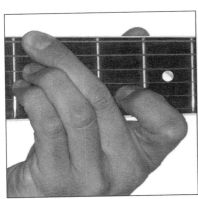
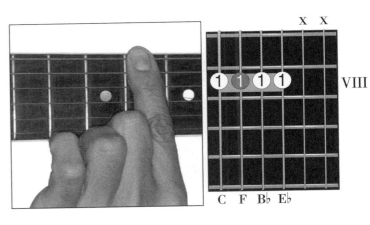

X X
VI
C B♭ E♭ F

X X
VIII
C F B♭ E♭

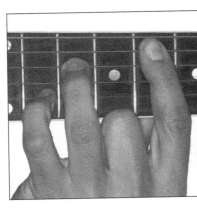
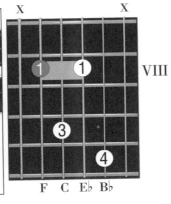 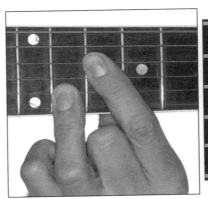

X X
VIII
F C E♭ B♭

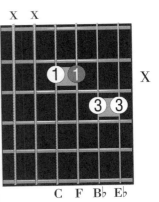

X X
X
C F B♭ E♭

F7♯11

F7♯5

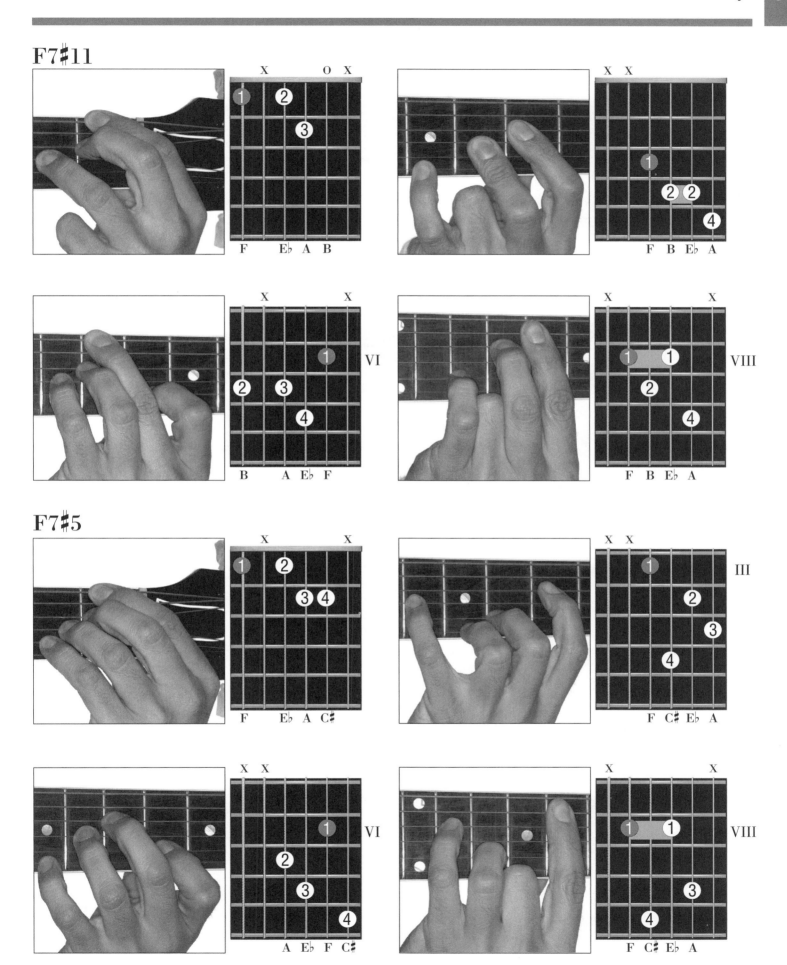

F9

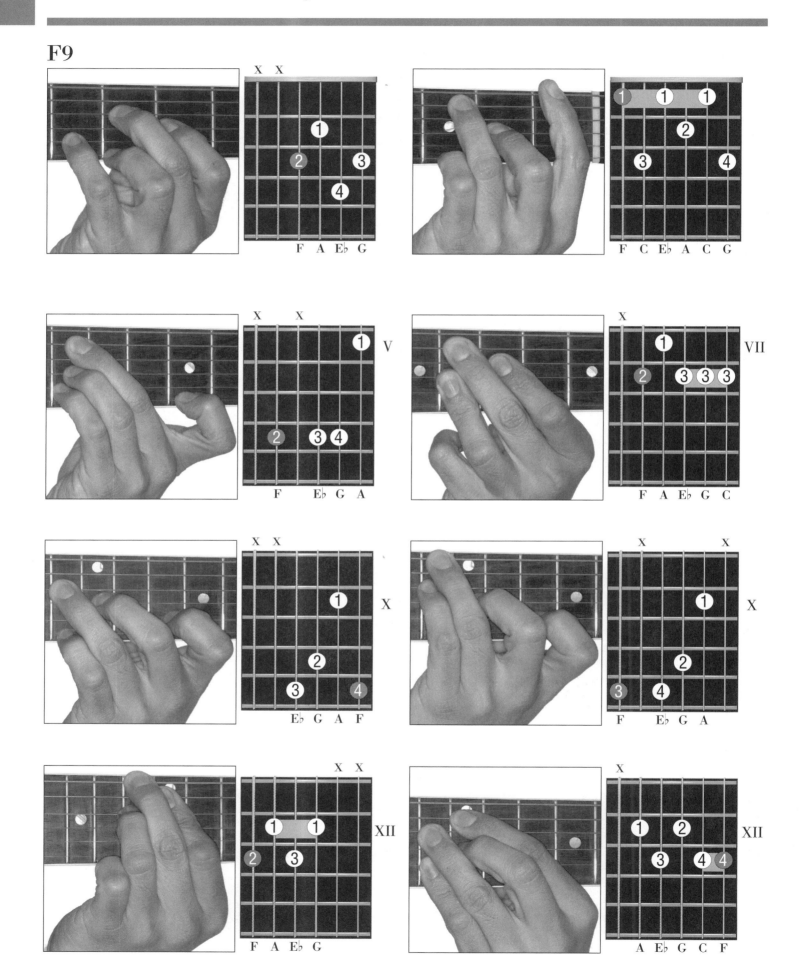

F9sus4

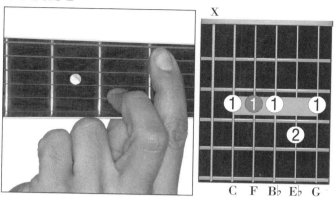

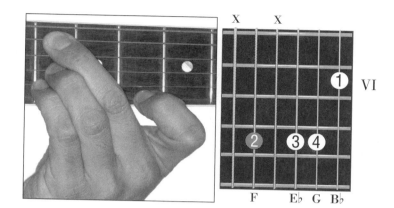

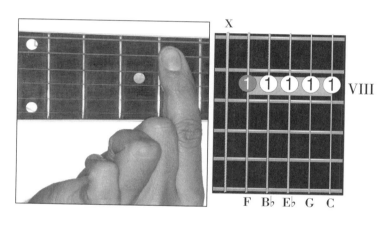

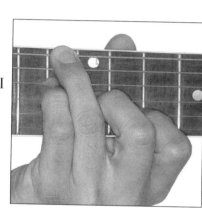

F9#11

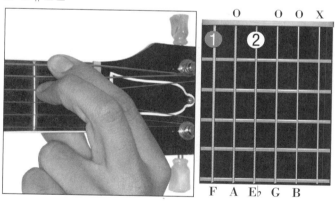

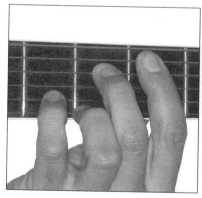

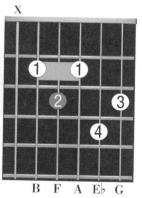

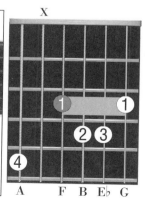

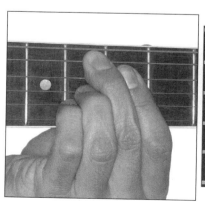

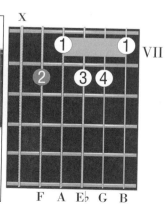

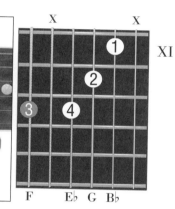

F9#5

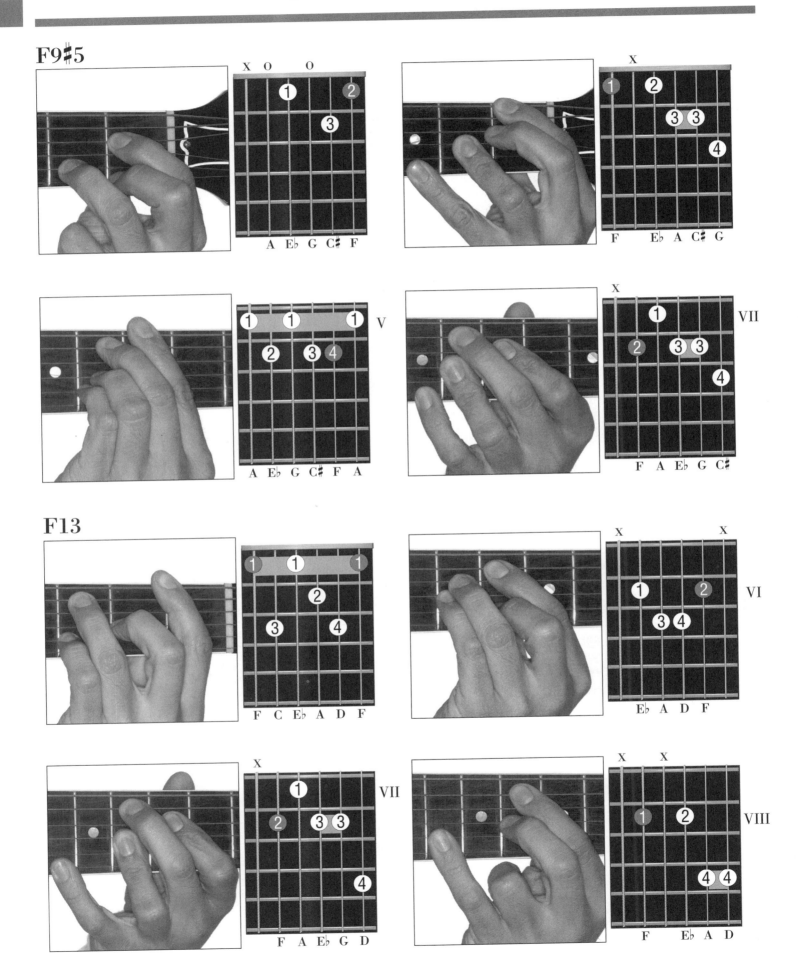

A E♭ G C# F

F E♭ A C# G

A E♭ G C# F A   V

F A E♭ G C#   VII

F13

F C E♭ A D F

E♭ A D F   VI

F A E♭ G D   VII

F E♭ A D   VIII

F13 *(continued)*

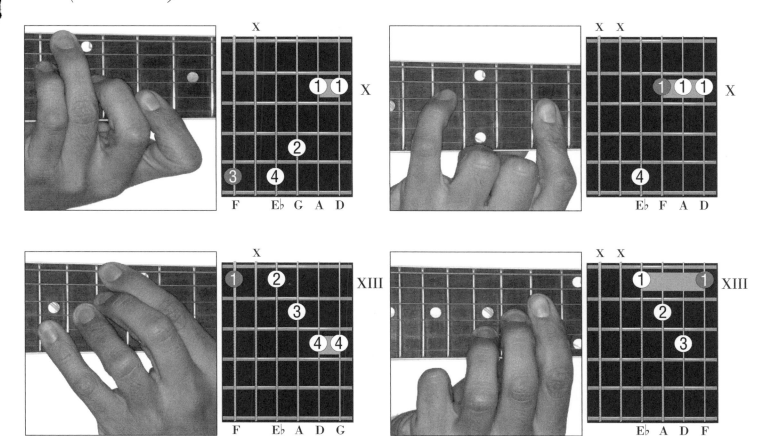